ANSWERS TO THE

TOP 20

INTERVIEW

QUESTIONS

CONQUERING THE JOB
INTERVIEW PROCESS

CERTIFIED CAREER COACH

KATIE WEISER

Disclaimer: The information and recommendations in this book are presented in good faith and for general information purposes only. Every effort has been made to ensure the materials presented are accurate, that the information presented is current and up-to-date at the time of printing, and Web addresses were active at the time of printing. All information is supplied on the condition that the reader or any other person receiving the information will do their own due diligence and make their own determination as to its suitability for any purpose prior to any use of this information. The purpose of this material is to educate. The author, Katie Weiser, and any affiliated companies shall have neither liability, nor responsibility to any person or entity with respect to any loss or damage caused or alleged to have been caused, directly or indirectly, by the information contained in this book.

ISBN-13: 978-1544166506
ISBN-10: 1544166508

Cover Design: Alex Tibio
Printed by: CreateSpace, An Amazon.com Company

Katie Weiser Coaching
www.katieweisercoaching.com
katie@katieweisercoaching.com

Printed in the United States of America

How Would You Answer the Top 20 Job Interview Questions?

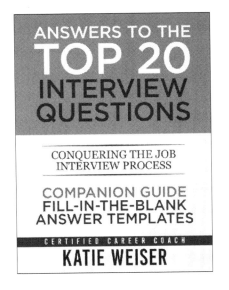

Are you worried about being tongue tied during the interview? Use the super-easy downloadable fill-in-the-blank COMPANION GUIDE ANSWER TEMPLATES for each of the Top 20 questions. Each template provides prompts to help you complete your own answers.

Your key benefits are:

- Knowledge of the prospective questions will give you a head start over the other candidates.

- The simple act of writing out your own answers will help you remember what you want to say.

- Advance preparation will reduce your anxiety and build your confidence.

- Your own answers captured on paper will enable you to rehearse and evaluate how well you are prepared.

Go to katieweisercoaching.com/top20/ to request your FREE downloadable fill-in-the-blank answer templates now!

DEDICATION

This book is dedicated to the two men in my life who encouraged my vision of helping others interview smarter. I am truly grateful for your patience and support from first words to finished manuscript.

With love and affection to my husband, Allan
AND
In loving memory of my brother, Walter Wade...you are truly missed.

CONTENTS

FOREWORD

"My palms were sweating, my knees were buckling, and I was clueless about what questions were going to be asked. My voice quivered with each answer, and my mouth was dry and scratchy. It seemed like the interview went on forever, and I was being judged from head to toe. When the interview was over, I got sick to my stomach and felt so defeated." Katie Weiser — my first job interview as a clerk-typist with the US Federal Government, Fort Richardson, Alaska

Are you trying to get ready for a job interview, but are wondering what questions are going to be asked? If you answered yes, then this is the perfect book for you! I'm Career Coach Katie Weiser, and I work with hundreds of clients each year to get them ready for their job interviews. I have kept a record of the most often asked questions from client feedback, and have narrowed it down to the Top 20 contained in this book. I get great satisfaction when clients come back to tell me that many of the Top 20 questions that we worked on together were asked and they felt prepared and ready to answer them. Even better news is that they got the job! Before we start, let me share a shocking statistic with you: the average person spends less than 60 minutes preparing for an interview. You might be surprised that this is not enough time. In my opinion, 60 minutes is just winging it and it will not get you the job. You need to prepare in advance and devote the time and effort it takes to become interview ready. So, congratulations to you for making the commitment to spend time upfront to be prepared with your answers to these interview questions. You will benefit greatly from the interview strategies I teach my clients. Let others wing it, so you can shine.

Preparing your answers in advance will reduce your anxiety and increase your confidence. Now, will you continue to be nervous before the interview? Of course, you will be. Butterflies in your stomach are perfectly normal. In fact, I firmly believe that if you aren't nervous, it means you don't really care. Those little butterflies and increase in adrenaline are natural.

So, how do we get you job interview ready so you can land the job you deserve? We will do this by:

1. Providing you with an understanding of the interview process.
2. Revealing to you the Top 20 interview questions and providing actual answers that my clients have perfected after my critique and mock interview.
3. Teaching the STAR (Situation, Task, Action, and Result) method of storytelling.
4. Providing you with some bonus interview tips.

The hours you devote to reading this book and crafting your own answers will provide you with a winning approach to make you a top candidate. It's my pleasure to be your coach through this book. If you're ready, let's get started.

CHAPTER 1

The Interview Process

Interviews can be nerve wracking for the job candidate. Nerves set in; physical symptoms appear like a dry mouth, sweaty palms, shaking hands, and a quivering voice. You feel uncomfortable under the discerning eye of the interviewer and feel like you are being judged. Negative thinking pops into your head that you aren't good enough, and you begin to question whether they can see through to your insecurity. On the flip side, interviews are time consuming for the employer. Hours of time go into the coordination and execution of interviews. Each hour a company employee spends in the interview process results in loss of productivity. Every wrong candidate hired, costs the company revenue. Thus, it only makes sense that they maximize the time and ask the questions needed to determine if someone is the right candidate or not.

In this chapter, I will help you understand the interview process. This will provide a foundation before we delve into the Top 20 questions individually. We are going to cover three topics:

1. How to view the interview as an opportunity to gain more clarity about the company and the job.

2. How to do company research in advance so you can be better prepared when you walk in the door.

3. Understanding the different kinds of interviews, the methods used to conduct the interview, and the types of question formats you may encounter. We don't want any surprises!

OPPORTUNITY

I would like you to think of the interview as a conversation between two people trying to get to know one another better. It's an opportunity for the employer:

- To explain the role and job description in more detail.

- To evaluate your skills relative to the job, your communication skills, how you think on your feet, your judgment, as well as your personality and attitude.

- To describe future opportunities and maybe even discuss your potential career path to see if you would be interested in joining them.

And, it is a great opportunity for you:

- To expand the interviewer's understanding and appreciation of your skills. A one or two page resume can't possibly capture the essence of who you are.

- To understand the company's culture—it could be laid back or more formal. Do they promote from within, and how do they treat their people? I always suggest arriving 15-20 minutes early so you can observe how employees interact in the reception area. Are they snarly with one another or are they supportive? Are they smiling and laughing? Does the company have values that match yours? Listen carefully as they discuss their mission and values with you.

- To determine whether you like what you heard when they talked about their company and future opportunities. Are they a good match for you?

COMPANY RESEARCH

The interview is an important opportunity for you to show your knowledge of the company by doing company research. Employers will want to know that you have taken the time to know a lot about them when you walk in the door. Thus, it is critical that you do your homework in advance. There is so much you can find by doing an Internet search, reading the company's website and checking your local newspaper for:

- Company history and current news

- Mission Statement, Values, Guiding Principles

- Number of employees, how many offices, where are they located, what has been their earnings progression, are they privately owned, publicly traded, or a family business?

- What are their main businesses/divisions—what do they manufacture, sell or do?

- Industry trends—what are some of the current issues they face?

- Who is their competition?

- Who works there? Use both LinkedIn and Facebook to see if you have friends who either work there or have in the past. If you find one, then take the time to talk with them about the company culture, the job opportunity and any other information that would be helpful. If none of your friends have worked at the company, ask them who they know who might work there. If they do know someone there, ask your friend if they would be willing to provide an introduction. Two questions I want you to ask them:

  1. Why do you like working here?
  2. Why do you stay?

Both answers will give you insight into the company values and how they treat their employees. You will also want to research:

- Common salaries for the job in your area. My two favorite sites to check out company salaries are: <u>Salary.com</u> and <u>Glassdoor.com</u>. I recently had a client who was an engineer and wanted to know the salary range for a large aerospace company. He was able to find the range on glassdoor.com for his city. It is pretty cool to know the salary before you have to answer, "What salary are you looking for?" In some cases, you may not be able to get the information, but you can research the job title on <u>Payscale.com</u>

- Check to see what awards they have won or any special recognition they have received. You can research how they were rated by Fortune magazine or local newspapers as "one of the best places to work." I recently did a speech and mentioned that I noticed the company was voted one of the best companies to work for in Augusta, GA. The room broke out into a loud cheer. Obviously, they were very proud of their accomplishment. You can also read up on whether they have done charity work. Mentioning their awards or charity work will score you points!

INTERVIEW METHODOLOGY

Next, it is important for you to understand the different kinds of interviews, interview methods used, and the question formats you may encounter. I lump these together under interview methodology.

Kinds of Interviews

There are three basic kinds of interviews: telephone, video/Skype or in-person.

1. **Telephone interviews** are usually a method to reduce the number of candidates they are going to bring in for one-on-one interviews—particularly for those living out of town. This makes sense to cut down on travel costs that they would incur to bring you to their location. The disadvantage is they can't see you. I suggest you stand as you will have better voice projection and will appear more confident.

2. **Video/Skype interviews** are also used to weed people out. The disadvantage here is you can't stand or walk around to relieve some of the tension. You are glued to your computer or Smartphone camera. A few tips: be sure the technology is working, sit upright so the camera can get a close up from the waist up, and look at the camera as opposed to the interviewer so that eye contact is crisp.

3. **In-person interviews** are an indicator of a strong interest in you. It is the objective of both telephone and video/Skype interviews to land an in-person interview next.

All kinds of interviews are nerve wracking! Advance preparation can include visualization techniques, stretching exercises, ensuring that you have a copy of your resume in front of you, a glass of water (no ice as that constricts the vocal chords), and pen and paper to take notes. Make sure your desk space looks neat, and you have a quiet place to talk. No coffee shops or children running around in the background.

Interview Methods
There are three types of interview methods:

1. **Sequential** – meaning a number of interviews. These could be scheduled on the same day or over a series of days or weeks. Often, it starts with a pre-screen interview with either a recruiter, or a human resources professional. Then, it often moves to the person you will be reporting to. I recently had a client who felt he had gone through the meat grinder after five interviews over a series of days. However, please know that if you are still in the running, you will progress from one interview to the next.

2. **Panel interview** – each panel member will ask you questions and then the panel will meet afterwards to determine who they believe is the best candidate. Please remember to look at all the panel members when answering questions, not just the member who asked you the specific question.

3. **Group** – a group is given a problem to work on as a team. Evaluators will be looking for your leadership and communication abilities and observe how you work in a team. The group dilemma shows how you stand out compared to your peer candidates.

Every company has a different process or combination of interview methods. Please be patient going through the paces. Afterwards, think about what you learned and would do differently in your next interview should you not get this job.

Question Formats

The average interview is 40 minutes. There are three basic question formats: job skill related, situational and behavioral. Let's review each one.

1. **Job skill related** – based on your past experience, would you be a good fit for them? Basically, this is how your resume got you in the door. They will want to dig deeper into your skill set.

2. **Situational** – the interviewer will ask questions that relate to a situation they are experiencing and want you to solve. For example: we are having difficulty managing our team productivity. How would you handle that? Here they are getting free advice from you and looking to see how creative you are with a new spin they have not thought of, or they are comparing your answers to others they have heard.

3. **Behavioral** – they will ask you how you handled a certain situation. This helps the employer predict how you will react, because they believe past performance is an indicator of future performance. For example: have you ever seen someone do something unethical... what did you do about it? Or tell me about a decision you made that was not popular... what did you do?

You could get asked a combination of these three types of questions. Also, another interview format you want to be aware of is: some companies will administer a personality assessment to help determine if you are the best fit for the job. They could use tried-and-true tests like the Myers Briggs or DISC, or they may have developed their own. My advice is to answer these assessments with your gut reaction. Don't over-think the questions. You want to be your true, authentic self when answering.

RECAP

Think of your interview as a conversation to get to know one another. It is a great opportunity to expand further upon your competencies and skills and to learn more about the company. Shine early on by doing your company research homework. Expect that you could have a telephone, video or an in-person interview or a combination of these. Be prepared for interviews that are one-on-one sequentially or conducted by a panel evaluating you or you may be observed in a group of your peers. Be ready for a combination of questions that can be job related, situational or behavioral. And, be sure to answer personality assessment questions with your gut reaction response. These are the foundational elements of the interview process.

"The only place opportunity cannot be found is in a closed-minded person." Bo Bennett, Author

CHAPTER 2

Know What You Offer

Being able to articulate who you are through your experience begins with knowing what you offer the employer. What is your value? How do you hook them from the beginning, so they stay engaged in the conversation? We will cover three pieces of the equation: know your strengths, know your brand and know the role you are applying for.

KNOW YOUR STRENGTHS

In an interview, you must be able to discuss your strengths in a coherent manner and with enthusiasm and pride. But, we often fumble, because strengths are so innate, and we take them for granted. Let's take a two prong approach to identifying your strengths:

1. A strength is defined as the combination of your knowledge, skills, and talent. Think about several jobs, tasks, projects that you have done in the past with great success. What are the strengths you used at the time? Take a moment to capture these below:

_____

_____

_____

_____

_____

_____

_____

_____

_____

2. If you are struggling with identifying your strengths, I suggest you purchase an excellent, yet inexpensive book on Amazon: StrengthsFinder 2.0 by Tom Rath. It costs about $15. In the back of the book is an envelope with a unique code to access an online assessment that will identify your Top 5 strengths. It won't take more than 20 minutes to complete—and remember when taking an assessment, answer with your gut reaction; don't over-think. These Top 5 strengths will prompt you to think of your work experiences in terms of strength themes.

Now that you have identified your strengths, pull out the job description—do your strengths match those listed in the job requirements? If you answer "yes", then these will be the strengths to enumerate throughout the interview and, in particular, for answering Question #4 – What Are Your Strengths?

KNOW YOUR BRAND

Your strengths come to life as part of your branding. I have created an exercise sheet for you called the Four Boxes of Personal Branding. While the strengths box is the most important, you can describe yourself with the words you place in the other three boxes. Your strengths are then couched in dialogue that is more conversational, engaging and memorable. Let's briefly describe each of the four personal branding boxes:

1. **Your Passions.** Are you a stickler for details and is everything you do almost error free? Do you have a passion for the mission of the company? Does people development make your heart sing?

2. **Personal Attributes.** What characteristics do you bring to the job that would be attractive to an employer? Integrity, punctuality, honesty, you are a team player, etc.

3. **Strengths.** The combination of your knowledge, skills and talents.

4. **Differentiators.** How are you different from other candidates? Do you speak a foreign language, have you played competitive sports that taught you the importance of teamwork, are you the eldest of six children who learned early on how to manage others? Are you a parent who respects work/life balance of your direct reports? Of course, the differentiator would need to be important to the employer.

You will want to weave these four dimensions into the conversation as you tell stories of your experience. More on storytelling later.

KNOW THE ROLE

I will keep emphasizing one thing—be sure to know the role, responsibilities and what they are looking for—scour that job description. Your strengths and your overall brand story must be tied to the employer's need. Ideally, you want to meet at least 80 percent of the requirements. Sometimes, it may indicate bachelor's degree or master's degree preferred. This does not mean you are out of the running if you do not meet their education requirements. I say go for it, if you meet the 80 percent rule. The other 20 percent should be responsibilities that you can learn on the job.

RECAP

The four brand box exercise allows you to see, at a glance, what you bring to the role. The passion, personal attributes and differentiators you have captured personalize your strengths. Using these descriptive words, matched to the job role and responsibilities, will make you stand out.

"Know thyself"...from the walls of the temple of Apollo at Delphi

The Four Boxes of Personal Branding

Passions	Personal Attributes

Strengths	Differentiators

CHAPTER 3

Question #1: Tell Me a Little About Yourself

Interviewers love to start the conversation with: "Tell me a little about yourself." It isn't really a question and it could mislead you to think that this is just small talk. Heads up... your two minute response often determines if the interviewer wants to continue the dialogue. This statement is the #1 interview question. This question could also be disguised as: "Tell me about your background." So, be prepared for either question. You will answer it the same way.

ANSWER TIPS

I realize that it can be intimidating to talk about yourself immediately. But, it is also a great opportunity for you to begin strong and shine. This response should be a quick two minute summary. Here is the formula to use to get this two minute opener prepared:

I want you to think in four distinct chunks: Who, What, Why, and then end with a Question.

1. **WHO:** Who you are which can encompass all your experience— a one to two sentence summary.

2. **WHAT:** Here you are going to showcase your expertise. Look at the skills you have that match the skills they are looking for. Go back to your previous exercise notes on what you believe you offer. Begin with those skills, your knowledge and talent. Think in terms of how the company will benefit from them.

3. **WHY:** Explain why you are interviewing with this company.

4. **QUESTION:** Finally, ask the interviewer a question that sets them up to tell you what they want to hear from you and gives you time to breathe! Otherwise, there could be an awkward pause between the two of you.

Let's take a look at some examples of how to craft the: Who, What, Why and Question for the interviewer.

EXAMPLES

New graduate or no job experience: My background to date has been centered around preparing myself to become a media specialist. Let me tell you how I have prepared myself. I graduated from XYZ College with a Master's in education with a specialization in library science. My past experience has been in a volunteer position at our local county library, helping patrons research projects and school papers. I have enjoyed using my strengths of working with people and directing them to the appropriate resources. I am here today because I am excited about the opportunity of working with such a highly-rated high school. What else would be helpful to know about me? (This puts the interviewer back in control by telling you what they want to hear).

Here they followed the formula: Who, What, Why, Question. **Who:** they were a student. **What:** they have been a volunteer in a library setting. **Why:** the school is highly-rated. **Question:** what else would be helpful to know about me? If you are a new graduate or new to the workforce, both part-time and volunteer work should definitely be on your resume.

Experienced Hire: I have 10 years of selling experience in the medical device field. I have spent the last seven years with Medical A Company where I sell mesh for surgical procedures. I have exceeded my sales quota every year—last year by $1 million and I was awarded sales person of the year. I am particularly interested in this position because you indicated that you are looking for aggressive sales leaders. With my base of contacts in hospitals and with doctors, I already have a ready sales pipeline that I can tap into. Although I enjoy my current position, I feel that I am ready to sell larger medical equipment and this position excites me. What else can I share with you?

Again the formula: **Who:** sales professional. **What:** here he was able to elaborate on what he sells—surgical mesh and he added metrics—exceeding his quota by $1 million. This ties in beautifully with the aggressive sales leader they are looking for. **Why:** selling in a bigger sandbox of medical equipment. **Question:** what else can I share with you?

Experienced Hire: I am a human resource professional with 15 years of experience specializing in training and development. I have spent the last three years in a professional services firm leading the learning practice of eight people to develop over 500 e-learning programs. We won several awards for innovative design and delivery on a mobile platform. I love leading the team, being on the cutting edge and working with firm leaders to deliver the training that will help their employees excel. I am excited by the opportunity here because of your international focus involving different cultures. I am fluent in French and Spanish. What else can I share with you?

Again the formula: **Who:** human resource professional. **What:** specialty in training and development—15 years is significant and qualifies for a leadership position. **Why:** company has an international focus and they could use the French and Spanish language capability. **Question:** what else can I share with you?

RECAP

Clearly tell **WHO** you are by summarizing your past experience, **WHAT** are your major strengths that tie into what the company is looking for, and then a quick **WHY** you are interested in the position. Then finally ask the interviewer a simple **QUESTION** like: **what else can I share with you?** This eliminates the awkwardness of whether you keep talking or they intercede. You want them to start asking you more questions. The advantages of this Who, What, Why, Question approach is that they will want to know more about you. You have taken one step forward to distance yourself from the other candidates.

Everyone kept telling me, just be yourself. Be yourself. I kept thinking, there's got to be more to it than that!
Tony Danza, Actor

Okay, your turn. Write out your answer to Question #1: "Tell me a little about yourself" on the next page or on the downloadable answer template.

1. Tell Me a Little About Yourself

WHO: Who you are which can encompass all your experience—a one to two sentence summary:

_____

_____

_____

WHAT: Showcase your expertise. Look at the skills you have that match the skills they are looking for. Go back to your previous chapter notes on what you believe you offer. Begin with those skills, your knowledge and talent. Think in terms of how the company will benefit from them.

_____

_____

_____

WHY: Explain why you are interviewing with this company.

_____

_____

_____

QUESTION: Finally, ask the interviewer a question that sets them up to tell you what they want to hear from you and gives you time to breathe! Use one of these:

• What else can I share with you?

• What else would be helpful to know about me?

CHAPTER 4

Question #2: Why Are You Looking for a Job?

Even though you already stated why you are interested in joining their company, they may ask you again: "Why are you looking for a job or leaving your current job?" They are fishing to see if you have performance problems or issues with your boss or co-workers. You might have been fired or downsized. How you handle the question says a lot about you as a person. Are you a complainer, a whiner, a gossip, or someone on an upward trajectory? Obviously, you want to grow and advance in your career. Be careful not to sound too cocky. Take the high road and answer the question honestly. Only you know the reason you want to leave. Avoid bad-mouthing your boss or co-workers. This will be a real red flag to them, thinking that you could repeat this behavior at their company. Let's face it, you never know who may know your boss or co-workers, and if it got back to them, you would be burning your bridges. If you were downsized, be positive and let them know it was strictly a business decision and that you were one of several or one of many. We will devote a separate chapter on how to explain "I was fired." Also, it is not a good idea to talk about wanting to earn more money. This is very bad form, because research shows that job satisfaction has less to do with money and more to do with challenge and continuous learning. Let's face it—the interviewer knows you want to earn more!

ANSWER TIPS

The best answers I have heard in all my years of interviewing candidates have to do with the following reasons, all very legitimate and understandable.

- Too much travel or my commute is too long.

- I am looking for more career challenge.

- My spouse or partner is being relocated to this city/town.

- I have topped out for promotion at my current company.

- My company is unstable and going under. Do not mention this if it is not already public news. Don't disclose anything confidential.

- I just graduated from college or am returning to the workforce.

EXAMPLES

Travel/Commute: My commute is one hour each way and I would welcome the opportunity to work at a company closer to home, so that I can devote those gained hours to work or time with my family.

Career Challenge: I enjoy my job and my contributions are appreciated; however, I want increased responsibility and challenge. I know this job offers this and your company is a leader in the industry. (Always mention something that you have researched about the company).

Relocation: My spouse just accepted a terrific job at XYZ Company in New York. This move gives me an opportunity to find a new position in a great city. We are already enjoying what the city offers.

Promotion Limits: I've reached the top of the ladder at my current organization, which is small in size. I appreciate all the experience it has afforded me. However, I believe it is time to move to a company which is larger and more complex and offers more challenge.

Unstable Company: I am sure you have read in the newspapers that my company is experiencing financial problems, and I am ready to be proactive in leaving. It was a great place to gain the skills I believe I can bring to this company.

New Graduate/Return to Work: I have just graduated/I have just finished raising my children and I am eager to join/rejoin the workforce. Your company and this job stand out for me as I believe it is a good match for my skills. I appreciate the opportunity to be here today.

RECAP

Be honest with your answer. You should be able to use one of the most common reasons for leaving. Using the career challenge reason is great. But, it's important to notice that I did not use the word "new challenge" in the example. The word "new" connotes that you will get bored and the interviewer might think you are not going to stay around a long time. Use the words, "more challenge."

"Keep calm and find a better job." Anonymous

Okay, your turn. Write out your answers to Question #2: "Why are you looking for a job?" on the next page or on the downloadable answer template.

 ## 2. Why Are You Looking for a Job?

Only you know the answer to this question. Be sure to be honest, don't bad-mouth bosses, colleagues or a company.

Write your answer:

_____

_____

_____

_____

_____

_____

Most common reasons:

1. Too much travel or commute is too long

2. Looking for more career challenge

3. Spouse or partner is relocating to the new city

4. Have topped out for promotions at current company

5. The company is unstable and going under (this would have to be public news)

6. Just graduated from college or returning to the workforce

CHAPTER 5

Question #3: Have You Ever Been Terminated?

"Have you ever been terminated" is a common question, so please don't feel you are being singled out. It is a straightforward question. Often, it is couched as right sized, downsized or just plain fired. If you have never been terminated, you can skip this chapter because you can honestly answer, "No, I have not been fired." But, if you have been terminated, you will want to tell the story in an honest and factual way and you want to stay composed.

ANSWER TIPS

First of all, when there are dips in the economy, lots of companies let people go. You may have been one of the casualties and that is an understandable excuse for being fired or downsized. There are also all sorts of reasons for being fired that have nothing to do with the economy. It happens. How you answer the question will provide useful information about problems you have encountered. The best way to answer the question is with grace and honesty. Be careful not to show bitterness and anger or bad-mouth your employer or ex-boss. Because only you know the details surrounding the dismissal, it is difficult for me to give you a stock answer. The key to your answer is the lesson you have learned from being fired. Think about your experience and determine what you learned and how it has changed your behavior.

EXAMPLES

Not on Time: I was fired because I was not able to get to work on time. I was taking care of my mother, who had broken her hip, and I had to get her to the hospital every morning at 8 am for therapy. My work start time was 10 am, but because the doctor's office was not running on schedule, I was late most of the time. I can understand my employer's point of view as they were counting on me to be on time. The medical process took two months and they were not able to accommodate my schedule. If something like this happened in the future, I would definitely talk with my employer in advance so we could work out a mutually workable schedule.

Downsized: I was fired because I was part of a downsizing of our entire department. The company decided to outsource our group overseas. I loved working for the company, but appreciate that they were trying to cut their costs. I am anxious to start fresh with a new company with my human resource skills.

RECAP

My advice: tell your story—don't be bitter, always see it from the employer's point of view and reveal how the experience has changed how you would handle the situation in the future.

"There's nothing wrong with being fired." Ted Turner

Okay, your turn. Write out your answers to Question #3: "Have you ever been terminated?" on the next page or on the downloadable answer template.

3. Have You Ever Been Terminated?

Tell your story—don't be bitter, always see it from the employer's point of view and reveal how the experience has changed how you would handle the situation in the future.

Write your answer:

_____

_____

_____

_____

_____

_____

_____

_____

_____

_____

CHAPTER 6

The Story Method

Interviewers love to ask questions that help them understand if you have had past experiences that would be relevant to the job you have applied for. We mentioned these earlier as behavioral type questions. Listen for questions that begin with: "tell me about a time when," "describe a situation," "how would you handle," and "give me an example when..." These behavioral questions are perfect to answer with a story using the STAR technique. This technique has been widely discussed on the Internet and does not seem to be attributable to any one person. I have developed the templates in this book to make it simpler for you to write out your answers.

STAR Technique (Situation, Task, Action, and Result)

Jennifer Aaker, professor of marketing at the Stanford Graduate School of Business, explains in a Stanford University blog post that stories are up to 22 times more memorable than facts alone. She demonstrates the importance of stories in shaping how others see you and as a tool of persuasion. By using success stories during your interview, the interviewer will remember your stories before facts, figures, or data. It also gives them an easy way to describe you to others in the organization. Let's take a look at an easy way to write your success stories using the STAR technique. Let's review this acronym:

- **SITUATION:** Describe the problem or opportunity you faced, just like a reporter who would ask the questions: who, what, where, when, why and how. This helps the interviewer understand the background. Let me use an example to explain this a little better. Say I am applying for a supervisory position and am asked: how have you handled an employee whose people skills were lacking? Here is how I would provide the situation background: Jane is an employee that I have supervised for three years and all of a sudden, I started getting complaints from her colleagues that she was being verbally abusive. It was affecting the team's productivity and morale.

- **TASK:** Explain what you had to do and the challenges you encountered such as a tight deadline, a sick employee, an inadequate budget, etc. Using our example about the employee with a lack of people skills, I would go into the task part of STAR like this: I knew immediately that my task would be to speak with Jane behind closed doors to ascertain why there was an abrupt change in behavior.

- **ACTION:** Explain what you did to solve the problem or how you met a performance objective by describing the process, steps, talent and strengths you used. This is where you start promoting yourself—modestly, of course. Now, back to our verbal abuse employee. During my private conversation with Jane, I asked her how things were going. She did not seem to want to talk and looked uncomfortable. So, I was direct with her and mentioned that the team wasn't functioning well and questioned if she knew why that was. Jane burst into tears. She said that she felt that she was in over her head, and everyone on the team was telling her what to do and she didn't like it. I thanked her for being honest and we continued the dialogue around her fears and lack of confidence and how we could get her up to speed with some tasks with which she was not comfortable. We also discussed how that could be frustrating to her colleagues. She actually admitted she had been the team grouch. So, with my coaching, communication and compassion skills, I was able to get the real story out of Jane and help her come up with a way to deal with her underlying problem—which was a skill problem—and then address her feelings of being criticized by the others.

- **RESULTS**: What was the outcome or bottom line result? How did your action make a difference? If you have metrics, please use them. Also, if you learned something through the experience, please share that, too. Back to our example. To tout my results I would say: Jane took to learning some new skills quickly, which raised her confidence, and she stopped yelling at her teammates. The bottom line is that I took a dysfunctional team and turned it back into a high-performing one, so that projects could be delivered on time and efficiently.

I encourage you to use this step-by-step STAR technique: Situation, Task, Action and Result to craft your success stories.

Tips

Your STAR story should sound like a well written story as opposed to wandering from fact to fact. Stories are also easier for you to remember. Limit your answer to three minutes—the focus is on you and your result. Stick to what you have written in your notes rather than ad-libbing or inventing as you go along. A well-rehearsed story will help differentiate you from other candidates. I will be using the STAR technique to answer a number of upcoming interview questions. Please use your downloaded Companion Guide answer templates with special prompts for each question requiring a STAR formatted answer.

"Be unpredictable, be real, be Interesting.
Tell a good story."
Barry Ritholtz, CIO of Ritholtz Wealth Management

The STAR Technique Template

SITUATION: Describe the problem or opportunity you faced:

_____

_____

_____

TASK: Explain what you had to do and the challenges you encountered:

_____

_____

_____

ACTION: Explain what you did to solve the problem or how you met a performance objective by describing the process, steps, talent and strengths you used:

_____

_____

_____

RESULTS: What was the outcome or bottom line result? If you have metrics, please use them. If there was a lesson learned, what was it?

_____

_____

_____

CHAPTER 7

Question #4: What Are Your Strengths?

Almost every interviewer will ask, "What are your strengths?" They want to know if the strengths you possess will align with the talent, skills, and knowledge they need for the job. Are you competent? This is not a time to be shy and retiring. You must be able to focus on the strengths that are most relevant to the job which you are applying for. You may also have strengths that are not a requirement of the new job, but make a point of focusing on the ones that are relevant. You must be articulate and confident as you answer the strengths question.

ANSWER TIPS

In Chapter 2, you created your list of strengths or took the Strengthsfinder 2.0 assessment to discover what your Top 5 strengths are. Compare and contrast your strengths and how they relate to the job description. Pick the top three that are part of the selection criteria for the new job. Make the connection for the interviewer even though it may be obvious to you. Your past work examples will demonstrate that you have the experience they are looking for. It could be from your current job or from a past job.

You don't want to do a full blown STAR story, but a modified version using only the A and R components: the Action and the Result. Also include components of your branding—one of those elements was strengths which addresses this question. The other three were passion, personal attributes, and differentiators. Adding one, or all three will make your statement much more memorable than going through the strengths you would bring. It is your brand—what you stand for and what you deliver time and time again.

Keep your responses to 60-90 seconds. Be sure to create several of these stories just in case they want you to elaborate on more skills.

EXAMPLES

New Graduate or No Experience: If you were applying for an administrative assistant position in a law office and the requirements were communication and organization skills, you could respond: I have been told by my friends that I am the go-to person for planning vacations. I write all the e-mail communications to advise of tour options, summarize the preferences, make the final choice of the tour of the day, collect the money to take advantage of group rates, and then advise everyone where they have to be on each day. Our trips run smoothly because of my abilities to organize and communicate. Everyone always says that I'm the one in charge next time.

Experienced Hire: If you were applying for a job where you were going to be a graphics design project manager and the job requirements were communication and leadership you could say something like this: I have been told that three of my strengths are my communication skills, creativity, and passion for leading teams. Recently, I was the project leader where I was managing several virtual graphic designers who were supporting a large advertising client. I made sure that everyone on the team was on the same page every Monday morning by conducting a Monday Milestone Call to review progress to date, deadline issues, staffing shortages, and then because I foster creativity, we ended each meeting with an open forum for creative problem resolution. This ended up being so helpful that the project was completed on time and we received accolades for creativity from the client, and bonuses were awarded to each team member by our company's president.

Notice that I did not use the words, "I believe my strengths are"... that could be interpreted as bragging. Instead, I started off my response with, "I have been told"... This is a great example by this graphics person. First, he described the ACTION he took which was

Monday morning meetings because it was a virtual team, and then he reported on the RESULT—client satisfaction and bonuses. In addition, he was able to add some branding to the story by expressing both passion and a differentiator. He has a passion for leading teams. Passion is a lot stronger than just strength alone. His differentiator was that he encouraged others to express their opinions in the open forum after each meeting (not all leaders would do this). It is a great indication of encouraging risk taking as well.

RECAP

Always begin by answering the question directly, and then tell your abbreviated story that showcases your skills. Remember, it is Action, Result, and add either something on passion, personal attribute or a differentiator to the story.

"Know your strengths and take advantage of them."
Greg Norman, Professional Golfer

Okay, your turn. Write out your answers to Question #4: "What are your strengths?" on the next page or on the downloadable answer template.

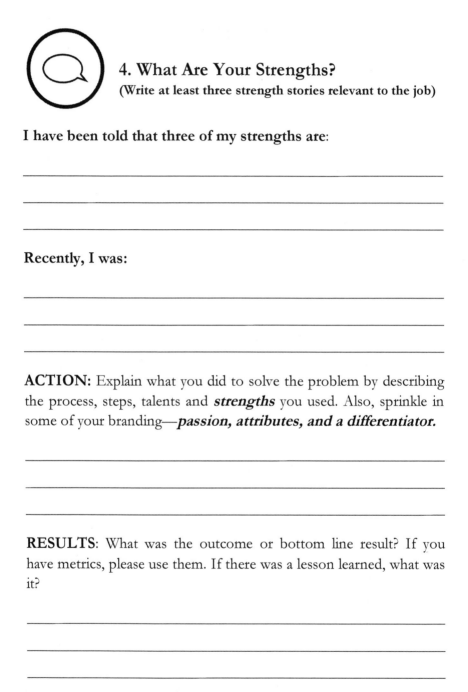

4. What Are Your Strengths?

(Write at least three strength stories relevant to the job)

I have been told that three of my strengths are:

_____

_____

_____

Recently, I was:

_____

_____

_____

ACTION: Explain what you did to solve the problem by describing the process, steps, talents and **strengths** you used. Also, sprinkle in some of your branding—**_passion, attributes, and a differentiator._**

_____

_____

_____

RESULTS: What was the outcome or bottom line result? If you have metrics, please use them. If there was a lesson learned, what was it?

_____

_____

_____

_____

CHAPTER 8

Question #5: What Are Your Weaknesses?

This is the flip side of the "what are your strengths" question. Believe me; we all have weaknesses, so you can't just answer, "I don't have any weaknesses." You must be prepared to answer this question and not look like a deer in the headlights when it is asked. Some interviewers ask the question just to trip you up—not nice, but it happens. In this instance, and with the pressure on, it is critical to have a well thought out answer. The interviewer will be looking to see if you have any self awareness—do you recognize a weakness in yourself? Can you articulate how you learned from it or overcame it? This kind of self reflection has to be done in advance so that you are prepared to answer the weakness question often disguised as, "If you could change one thing about yourself, what would it be?" They are fishing for a weakness here, too.

ANSWER TIPS

Honesty is always the best policy with the weakness question. Your response must strengthen your chance of getting the job as opposed to weakening it.

Here are a few tips for you:

- Be sure NOT to talk about a weakness that is a requirement for the job. Instead...

- Talk about a weakness that you have overcome or are actively working to change.

- Offer a weakness that is not important to the job.

Start your answer with a short description of the weakness and then discuss what you did or currently do to neutralize it.

EXAMPLES

No experience: You may think that because I am a recent college graduate/returning to the workforce and don't have work experience that this would be my greatest weakness. I believe that my willingness to do my best, coupled with my ability to learn new things quickly, will make me a fast study of your processes and procedures. I believe your organization will provide high-quality training to get me up to speed, and I will enjoy the challenge.

Experienced: In the past, I have taken on everything that has been given to me without question, and this has resulted in my being stretched too thin. I have had to learn the hard way to analyze the best use of my time by prioritizing it and then discussing it with my boss. Every time we review what is on my plate, she agrees to take something off in order for me to deliver a quality product. She appreciates my giving 100 percent to all my projects and identifying when there is too much work to be effective.

Experienced: I have a bias to action to get things done. I have always wanted to beat my deadlines to be ahead of schedule. But, sometimes, I drive the team too hard to accomplish this and it was pointed out to me by my supervisor. So, I still strive to beat the deadline, but have learned that the team morale is also important. I have learned that the team also has to buy-in to a timeframe. We do this by openly discussing each week how everyone is managing their piece of the project. If we find there are issues, we discuss how we can shift resources to ensure that we meet or beat deadlines. It has created more of a positive team attitude. So, for sure, the team rarely misses a deadline. I also know that when we are not able to beat a deadline, every team member has done their best and they have pulled together. And, if we do beat the deadline—it is just an added bonus.

RECAP

The weakness question may be the most important question after Question #1 – Tell Me a Little About Yourself. If the interviewer feels that you are trying to bluff or are spinning a tale, you might get nuked at this point in the interview.

"Our greatest weakness lies in giving up"
Thomas Edison, Inventor

Okay, your turn. Write out your answers to Question #5: "What are your weaknesses?" on the next page or on the downloadable answer template.

5. What Are Your Weaknesses?

In describing a weakness, remember to:

- Talk about a weakness that you have overcome.

- Offer a weakness that is not important to the job.

Short description of the weakness:

_____

_____

_____

_____

What did you do or are currently doing to neutralize the weakness?

_____

_____

_____

_____

_____

_____

_____

CHAPTER 9

Question #6: Tell Me About Any Previous Issues with a Boss

Watch this question. It is a double-edged sword because you never want to say negative things about a previous boss or a company. Keep in mind that any bad-mouthing will lead the interviewer to believe that someday you could be talking about them or their company in an inflammatory way. If you are interviewing in your hometown, news gets around fast and this interviewer might even know your prior boss. If you are bitter about a company or a boss, this is not the time to go on a diatribe. Interviewers want to see how you are going to discuss the situation and how you grew professionally from the conflict, disagreement or clash in values.

ANSWER TIPS

Saying you have never had any problems with a boss is unrealistic. We have all worked for jerks, but we learn from the bad bosses too. Your answer to issues with a prior boss needs to be honest, respectful and positive. The emphasis should be about how you tried to improve the relationship. This is at the heart of resolving all conflict—seeing it from the other person's perspective, coming to an agreement, and staying on task. This would be an excellent time to use the STAR model to answer the question.

EXAMPLES

Boss Blame: My relationship with my former boss was excellent. We were a great team and my boss knew he could trust me to get the customer invoices out on time. However, recently he blamed me for not being thorough because he had heard from some new customers that they had not received invoices for payment. When I was able to take the time to sit down with him to discuss that the new clients he listed were not in our client tracking system, we both knew that there had to be a bottleneck. We discovered that 15 new client accounts had not been set up by the accounting department because they were on the desk of an employee who was on vacation. I could appreciate my boss's reaction to thinking that the invoices had not been mailed. He had a lot to lose, about $30,000 in revenue, and it could become a collection issue. I am happy we were able to investigate the problem together and resolve it quickly. I learned that my calm demeanor worked in my favor because I did not take offense to the accusation of not mailing out the invoices.

This answer shows that you get along well with your boss, but also that you are not a shrinking violet when accused of something you did not do. You were proactive in identifying the root cause of the problem. It also indicates that whatever comes up between you and a boss, that your immediate reaction is to uncover what the true cause is. It also shows that you stick to your guns and don't take the blame for others. From a STAR perspective—we understand the SITUATION—the boss was upset about the new clients not receiving invoices; your TASK was to respond to your boss; your ACTION was to uncover the root cause, and your RESULT was finding out what actually happened and restoring the relationship to an even keel.

Boss Disagreement: I pride myself on getting along professionally with all my ex-bosses and my current boss. There are times when I may have disagreed with a boss's idea, but I have always felt comfortable to express my point of view. I believe that my bosses have viewed me as someone who is not a 'yes person' and that I will be honest and open, because it is part of my job. The result is that it helps the relationship to look at things from a different point of view. In the end, though, I am always supportive of whatever final decision the boss makes.

This answer shows that you have enough confidence to have a point of view (strength) and at the same time, you are supportive of the leader and do not do things behind their back, or bad-mouth them.

This example is a shorter STAR version: SITUATION: disagree with the boss. TASK: state your point of view. ACTION: implied is that you are courageous because you are honest and open. RESULT: You always support your leader.

RECAP

Conflict with a boss or co-worker is not an easy fix. Having the courage to discuss the issue openly and to work on a solution to resolve it shows the interviewer that you are an individual who values relationships and does not shy away from conflict. The emphasis is on collaboration. Even if you are a new college graduate or returning to the workforce, examples of conflict with friends, professors, or colleagues in volunteer or part-time jobs are also relevant.

"Conflict cannot survive without your participation."
Dr. Wayne Dyer, Author

Okay, your turn. Write out your answers to Question #6: "Tell me about any previous issues with a boss." on the next page or on the downloadable answer template.

6. Tell Me About Any Previous Issues with a Boss

The STAR Technique Template

SITUATION: Describe the problem or opportunity you faced *with your boss*:

_____

_____

TASK: Explain what you had to do and the challenges you encountered:

_____

_____

ACTION: Explain what you did to solve the problem or how you met a performance objective by describing the process, steps, talents and strengths you used.

_____

_____

_____

RESULTS: What was the outcome or bottom line result? If you have metrics, please use them. If there was a lesson learned, what was it?

_____

_____

CHAPTER 10

Question #7: How Would Your Manager or Co-Workers Describe You?

This question is about your ability to see how others view you. Sometimes, feedback from others can be enlightening, and at other times it confirms what you know about yourself. This question can also applaud you for how well you get along with your manager and co-workers. I know it is uncomfortable to talk about yourself, but you've got to toot your own horn here.

ANSWER TIPS

Here are several ways to jog your memory of how others describe you:

1. Take out your personal branding sheet to see if any of the words remind you of a quick story that demonstrates a passion, personal attribute, strength or differentiator, or a combination of 1-3 that you have heard others describe you as exhibiting.

2. You can also take a look at a recent performance appraisal from your boss or upward evaluation report. What were the strong positive comments?

3. Tell one of your success stories where you received positive feedback as your RESULT.

4. Bring letters of recommendation and/or LinkedIn endorsements.

EXAMPLES

Personal Branding: One thing I've noticed is that I'm always the go-to person for human resource problems. I listen carefully to the issues at hand and use my coaching skills to help the person come up with their own answer as opposed to my just telling them what to do. If you were to ask my colleagues, I believe they'd describe me as caring, understanding, and a great listener and mentor.

Performance Review: In my most recent performance review, my manager described me as someone who looks at all sides of a dilemma before I come to a conclusion. My role involves a lot of analysis and making the right choices equates to making money for our financial clients. I always look out for the company's best interests, and I know I am valued for this.

Success Story: Several years ago, we had to organize an office retreat for 100 people. We wanted to hold an evening dinner with a special event that was classy and private. It was my job to select the venue. I searched all over Miami for a great place to hold the event and found an Italian villa with formal gardens which was also a museum. The villa was available for rent. I worked with a catering company for all the table and chair rentals, a tent in case it rained, and the food. The dinner was set up on the back lawn overlooking the water. Our employees were greeted by a string quartet playing classical music during appetizers. We also hired a well-known comedian to entertain. My colleagues raved about the event and complimented me for my organization, creativity and design ideas. My boss would describe me as the total package, a detailed project manager who can turn a theme into reality. Since that event 10 years ago, I have been responsible for our annual meeting logistics.

Letters of Recommendation: If you have letters of recommendation, you can reference what has been said in them and hand it to the employer. Often, letters of recommendation are asked for after the fact, but be armed in advance to present them. It adds an ounce of credibility.

RECAP

Think in terms of your personal branding, a performance review, or a success story that you could be passionate about telling. Bring letters of recommendation as a leave-behind. Be proud and shine!

"Everyone likes a compliment." Abraham Lincoln, 16th U.S. President

Okay, your turn. Write out your answers to Question #7: "How would your manager or co-workers describe you?" on the next page or on the downloadable answer template.

7. How Would Your Manager or Co-Workers Describe You?

Time to Toot Your Own Horn – use one of these methods:

1. Use words from your personal branding sheet:

One thing that I have noticed is, or my colleagues tell me that:

_____

_____

_____

_____

2. Use positive comments from a recent performance appraisal:

In my recent performance review, my manager described me

as: _____

_____

_____

3. Tell a success story using the STAR Technique:

_____

_____

_____

_____

_____

_____

CHAPTER 11

Question #8: Describe a Situation When You Had to Meet a Challenging Deadline

We have all met challenging deadlines. They may have been self-imposed or not. Time and resources are usually the issues. Sometimes the date is simply unrealistic from the beginning. Other times, our clients or bosses say they want it sooner and we are left holding the ball. Team dynamics play into the equation when teams don't buy into the date or there is infighting. Often, we burn the midnight oil to get the work done and leave exhausted as we head out the door for a few hours of rest. After some sleep, you don't even want to get out of bed to face the mountain of work. Let's face it, deadlines create enormous stress. But, I am sure you will have a good story to tell of how you overcame a challenging deadline.

ANSWER TIPS

To make a good impression with regards to time, make sure you are prompt for your interview. There are no excuses for being late. If you get there a little early, even better. This already speaks volumes about how you manage your time. So, be on time.

Companies that work under tight deadlines often ask their applicants to describe a situation where they had a challenging deadline. They do this for two reasons:

1. To ensure you understand that they are a company with a culture of tight deadlines, and that your job will require the ability to take on pressure.

2. To determine if you can convince them that you can deliver your work and projects on time.

The deadline question focuses on planning the work and managing the resources. It makes sense to tell one or two short stories using the STAR method to describe how you overcame obstacles or people issues to meet a difficult deadline.

If you have primarily worked by yourself, you want to tell how you ordered the tasks that needed to be completed and then how you were able to overcome any obstacles to completing the project on time. Again, use the STAR method of storytelling.

The interviewer will be looking to see how you included your co-workers, whether you worked overtime, or worked at home. Basically, they want to see that you will do whatever it takes to get the job done.

EXAMPLES

Recent Graduate: I had to prepare a PowerPoint presentation for my college psychology class in under one week. I developed a timeline and listed all the activities I would need to accomplish it, such as research, creating a storyboard to support my premise and main points, creating the actual PowerPoint slides, searching for appropriate clipart and graphics online so that my slides would not be too wordy, planning for any rewrites or corrections, and then time to rehearse the presentation. It would take 40 hours to do it right. I knew it was impossible to get it done in the time I had available after working 20 hours a week and attending my other classes. I enlisted a friend to do the research and drop it off at my house in exchange for me doing the same thing for her in the future. By obtaining an extra resource, I was able to free up five hours of my time. As a result, it took me 35 hours instead of 40. The end result was that I was able to deliver a high-quality presentation on time.

Experienced Hire: Our financial closings are scheduled the last day of the month with reports due to the CFO the next morning. At my current job, I am responsible for our monthly financial closings. I have to summarize the data that comes in from sales representatives, but often the reps don't get their sales reports in until 5 pm. So, I work in the evening at home to get it done. My family knows that I have to reserve extra hours of my time, and they are very understanding about the hard work I put in each month to get the reports done on time.

Experienced Hire: Deadlines motivate me, particularly if they are deadlines with no wiggle room. Recently, we had to launch a new training program. The conference center had been booked in Scottsdale, Arizona. 120 participants had received their e-mail invites and the instructors were lined up. We had been down this path many times before and always delivered a seamless training program, but what made this deadline tough was the airlines lost all our training materials 48 hours before the first session was to start. There were only four of us on site. We quickly divided up the necessary tasks such as training binder reproduction, purchasing supplies, contacting vendors for reshipment of their materials, and printing nametags and welcome memos. We worked round the clock, ordered pizza for dinner and helped each other out. The result was another on-time, seamless program and the Director of Training was very impressed with what we had accomplished in such a short period of time.

RECAP

Projects are always subject to deadline-driven work. Often, it is unpredictable because of many variables. By using the STAR technique, your answer will be a memorable story that demonstrates to the interviewer that you are the right person to keep projects on track.

"A goal is a dream with a deadline."
Napoleon Hill, Author

Okay, your turn. Write out your answers to Question #8: "Describe a situation when you had to meet a challenging deadline" on the next page or on the downloadable answer template.

8. Describe a Situation When You Had to Meet a Challenging Deadline

The STAR Technique Template

SITUATION: Describe the *deadline,* problem, or opportunity you faced:

_____

_____

TASK: Explain what you had to do and the challenges you encountered:

_____

_____

ACTION: Explain what you did to solve the *deadline challenge* by describing the process, steps, talents and strengths you used:

_____

_____

RESULTS: What was the outcome...*did you meet the deadline or not? What did you learn?*

_____

_____

_____

_____

CHAPTER 12

Question #9: How Do You Deal with Pressure or Stressful Situations?

Companies want someone who is not going to shrink or freak out from situations that are stressful. The big question is: can you handle the pressure, including the pressure of the interview? Companies want people who can be like the quote you see everywhere—keep calm and carry on. They want to see how you manage stress and whether your great skills such as problem solving, time and people management, and decision-making may be affected negatively when you are put to the pressure test.

ANSWER TIPS

You can't just give a short answer of: yes, I handle stress well or I thrive under the pressure. It is too generic. Describe ways that you cope with stress. Think about the techniques you use to calm yourself. For me, I take some deep breaths while I close my eyes and try to clear my mind—my quick way of doing meditation. For some, it could be your strength of adaptability. For others, it could be taking a walk, exercising, or meditation. Give some thought to a recent stressful situation and think about how you coped and use the STAR story format.

EXAMPLES

Emotional control: In my job as a patient advocate at XYZ Hospital, I listen to angry patients every day who want resolutions to their problems. They often yell at me, which was very stressful and upsetting to me at first. I had to take control of my emotions and learn not to take it personally. I no longer put up a stressful wall of resistance. Instead, I have become a better listener and exhibit more empathy.

Stress reliever. I'm not easily rattled. In fact, my current boss calls me "the rock" because I don't get flustered easily. I have multiple projects to manage at one time and with all the variables, I find that the stress can cause overwhelm. When I find I am feeling stressed, I take a 15-minute walk around the office to clear my head. I feel the stress is relieved. When I get back to my cubicle, my head is cleared. I can then take the time to prioritize the many projects I am working on. I find that a little bit of exercise works for me, and I feel I am moving forward once again without all that stress.

Choice. Our department was recently audited by the IRS. This upset a lot of my co-workers, and my boss was pretty stressed out. As the accounting manager, the blame would sit squarely on my shoulders. I made a conscious choice not to be stressed out. I knew that our books were kept meticulously and that in the end, we would find out why we were being audited. I shifted any stress to the thought that if there were infractions, I would use it as a learning experience to understand how we could change some of our accounting practices. After four days, the IRS found nothing. Had I let the stress get the better of me, I would not have been cool, calm and collected and able to focus on the task at hand. We did learn that a disgruntled employee, who had been fired, had reported us out of spite to the IRS. My boss was thrilled that I was able to handle what he perceived as unbearable stress.

RECAP

The secret to telling your stressful story is to explain how you avoid the negative stress that can affect your productivity, which in turn affects the company. Explain how you meet stress head-on so the interviewer understands that nothing will stand in your way of getting the job done.

"A diamond is just a piece of charcoal that handled stress exceptionally well." Anonymous

Okay, your turn. Write out your answers to Question #9: "How do you deal with pressure or stressful situations?" on the next page or on the downloadable answer template.

9. How Do You Deal with Pressure or Stressful Situations?

The STAR Technique Template

SITUATION: Describe the *pressure or stressful situation* you faced:

_____

_____

_____

TASK: Explain what you had to do and the challenges you encountered:

_____

_____

_____

ACTION: Explain how you *coped with pressure and stress and the steps, techniques and strengths you used:*

_____

_____

_____

RESULTS: What was the outcome of *managing the pressure and stress? What have you learned by using this coping technique?*

_____

_____

_____

CHAPTER 13

Question #10: Tell Me About a Time When You Had to Work with a Difficult Person

There seems to be an epidemic of difficult people these days. You just want everyone to chill. But, that would be utopia. The workplace does hand us people who yell, are abusive, difficult, backbiting, immature, arrogant, unappreciative, uncooperative, very demanding, and downright unprofessional. This creates conflict at work and often leads to a toxic work environment.

I know you will have a great STAR story for this question. However, it is the manner in which you describe the situation and how you handled it that is key. The interviewer will be looking to see how you deal with these kinds of people—do you get emotional and create more turmoil, or do you find the diplomatic way of dealing with them? Or worse, do you put your head in the sand because you are not skilled at handling conflict?

ANSWER TIPS

Take the time before you go into your story to describe your philosophy of how to handle 'difficult' people in general. Things like truly listening to them often help to diffuse the situation. Asking the person how they would solve the problem empowers them to come up with their own solutions. Also, be sure to state that you do not tiptoe around the person. Taking charge and talking with the person immediately, in private of course, is the right thing to do. The conversation has to be about how you feel when they do xyz as opposed to putting the blame on that person.

EXAMPLES

Complainer: Working as a customer service representative for a national phone company, I receive a lot of complaints about our service. My responsibility in all these situations is to retain our clients and not have them leave us for another phone company. I recently had a man who was very upset that his Internet was not working for several days as he had a home-based Internet business that was losing money every day the Internet was down. I immediately acknowledged his issue and validated his emotions about his losing money daily. I assured him that I would stay with him until we got him back up and running. We were able to do a diagnostic and fix his problem. He was happy, but I also went one step further to ask him what else we could do to rectify the situation. He was so thrilled with the service; he thanked me and told me there was nothing else that needed to be done. Through my active listening and empathy, I came to really understand where the customer was coming from, and we turned an irate customer into a satisfied client.

If you work in the customer service industry, I want to share a great quote with you. It is from Stew Leonard's, a local grocery store in Norwalk and Danbury, Connecticut. Two rules are etched into a huge rock outside the entrances. Rule #1: The customer is always right. Rule #2: If the customer is ever wrong, re-read Rule #1. This is a great philosophy. What is your philosophy on customer service?

Saboteur: I recently had a colleague who was in a meeting I was leading. She began making derogatory comments to people next to her about how wasteful the meeting was. She did this while I was talking. I could feel others in the room were beginning to feel uncomfortable. I knew that if I did not say something, the meeting would be a total disaster. I also wanted to honor my philosophy that when people are difficult, they have a point of view or perspective. I politely, but firmly, asked her to state her opinions openly and we would discuss her comments. She began to back down and then made some worthwhile comments. After the meeting, I took her aside and asked her if there was anything in particular she wanted to say to me. She went into a complaint fest about meetings in general and how useless they were. I asked her for suggestions on how to make our meetings more productive and she offered up some ideas. I then told her that one of the derailers of meetings is side conversations. She turned beet red and realized that she was part of the problem. She apologized. Because she was so open, I began to ask her in advance to review our agendas and also to be our timekeeper. My ability to uncover what was upsetting her, respecting her as an individual with a perspective, helping her with self-awareness, and then including her in the solution, resulted in better run meetings with a more engaged co-worker.

RECAP

Think about your philosophy in dealing with difficult colleagues, clients, or employees. Craft a STAR story and wind up as someone who does not shy away from difficult people, but meets them head on.

"I am thankful for all the difficult people in my life. They have shown me exactly who I don't want to be."
Anonymous

Okay, your turn. Write out your answers to Question #10: "Tell me about a time when you had to deal with a difficult person" on the next page or on the downloadable answer template.

10. Tell Me About a Time When You Had to Deal with a Difficult Person

The STAR Technique Template

SITUATION: Describe the problem or opportunity you faced:

_____

_____

_____

_____

TASK: Explain what you had to do and the challenges you encountered:

_____

_____

_____

ACTION: Explain what you did *to work with the difficult person*:

_____

_____

_____

RESULTS: What was the outcome *based on your philosophy of working with difficult people?*

_____

_____

_____

_____

CHAPTER 14

Question #11: Describe a Situation When Your Work Was Criticized

Constructive criticism of your work is meant to be helpful. It is usually offered to point out mistakes or where you can make improvements. It may sting, but if you view it as a learning opportunity, you can use it to your advantage to become more proficient in a skill. An interviewer will want to see how you react to criticism and determine how you respond to being coached. Do you take it as a personal attack and go on the defense, do you feel demoralized, do you go into a corner and pout, or has it paralyzed you and is now affecting your job performance? Hopefully, none of these reactions apply to you. You want to show how you took the criticism to heart and made a change in your behavior—for the better.

ANSWER TIPS

This is a great time for another STAR story. Pick a story that is not a major mistake. Do not relate it to the weakness question previously. It needs to be a totally different story that deals with criticism. You must be able to describe constructive criticism that you responded to in a positive way, which led to improvement in your skills or a personal attribute. In the end, it contributed to your professionalism. Be sure to mention that it is no longer a problem for you because you took the advice, incorporated it, and now practice it regularly. Since no one is perfect, I know you have an ideal STAR story to tell.

EXAMPLES

Unsolicited Feedback: Our company has a lot of status updates on products. I am responsible for delivering at least one presentation a week. It takes a lot of preparation to determine my message, tailoring it to the audience and then doing the actual presentation. I completed my first presentation nine months ago and one of the participants came up to me afterwards and asked me if I wanted some feedback. I did not know the individual personally, but figured any helpful criticism is welcome. I invited her to share her thoughts. While she was mostly impressed with the flow of my presentation, she felt that I did not engage the audience with well-placed questions to see if they understood what I was saying or take time to solicit questions throughout the presentation as opposed to leaving them all to the end. It was certainly a different approach from what I had experienced when others presented, but I thanked her and said I would give it a try next time and would welcome her input in advance so we could place questions where she thought were most appropriate. She was so right! Now, my presentations are much more interactive and I can see the light bulbs go on when I include the audience in the solutions I am proposing.

Deadly Feedback: Two years ago, when I was new in my position working as an administrative assistant to our CEO, I was asked to attend a company board meeting with her. She asked me to take minutes. Fortunately, I was able to capture everything that was said and quickly type up the minutes. I left them in her inbox that night. The next morning, she came into my office and dropped the minutes on my desk with one word: "Unacceptable." I was taken aback a little bit, but composed myself to ask what was unacceptable and what she was asking me to do. She blurted out that she did not need word for word notes, only action items. I thanked her and said I would have it on her desk shortly, which I did. When I took the revision back to her, she said she liked the way I handled her and my gumption for just pressing on. I told her I appreciated that she explained exactly what she wanted so I could correct my mistake. I had made the error of assuming minutes meant verbatim, which was my experience in a law firm. Since then, we have gotten along great, and whenever she has something to teach me, she comes in and uses "Unacceptable" as the start of the dialogue, and I embrace it.

RECAP

How you handle criticism is a barometer of your willingness to accept feedback, whether it is constructive and with the best of intentions or it comes out of the blue unexpected and is delivered in a sarcastic way. It really is about adopting an attitude of gratitude that someone has actually taken the time to comment—positive or negative. View it as a gift. Be sure to express, in your own words, how you welcome feedback and criticism because it is a catalyst for your professional growth.

"Feedback is the breakfast of champions."
Ken Blanchard, Author

Okay, your turn. Write out your answers to Question #11: "Describe a situation when your work was criticized" on the next page or on the downloadable answer template.

11. Describe a Situation When Your Work Was Criticized

The STAR Technique Template

SITUATION: Describe *who offered the criticism and the manner in which it was done:*

_____

_____

_____

_____

TASK: Explain *what the criticism was about:*

_____

_____

_____

_____

ACTION: Explain *how you handled the criticism:*

_____

_____

_____

RESULTS: Explain *how the criticism improved a skill or personal attribute:*

_____

_____

_____

CHAPTER 15

Question #12: Tell Me About a Recent Accomplishment

Finally, the opportunity to talk about your greatness again! But, keep it focused on your professional experience. Even though your greatest accomplishment may be getting your 18-year-old to be self-sufficient or that you won the state track meet when you were in high school, this is not the time to talk about personal things. This question could be asked multiple times because it is truly what the interviewer wants to zero in on. Be prepared with at least three accomplishment stories from the last 18 months.

ANSWER TIPS

Great opportunity again for the STAR answer format. You can use examples from what you have listed on your resume—just expand upon them. This time you want three stories you are proud to tell.

Here are a few tips to help you generate these stories:

1. Focus on an accomplishment that is transferable to the job you are applying for. This makes you seem more qualified—a better fit. Things like process improvement, understanding of people issues, innovation or creativity, brainpower, or the ability to be strategic.

2. Mention your work awards if you have any—employee of the month, sales person of the year etc.

3. Talk about teamwork and your ability to be a team player or team leader. One caution, if you are a leader of a team, be sure to toot your own horn as opposed to giving all the credit to the team. I recently had a client who came to me after she did not get a job at

a large U.S. utility company. We discussed how she spoke about being the team leader. She gave all the accolades to her team and the interviewer actually stopped her to criticize that she, as the leader, did not seem to take responsibility for the team wins.

EXAMPLES

Award: Even though I do not have job experience, I volunteered to organize a 5K run for adoption. I was responsible for going out into the community to solicit sponsors for the event. I had to muster up the courage to knock on the doors of business owners, explain our goals, and the result of families receiving money to adopt kids. We engaged a website developer to create a site that would allow for runner registration and sponsor donations. I was able to sign up 25 sponsors who contributed over $40,000. I was thrilled that there were over 200 runners on the day of the race. It was a huge success and I received a letter of appreciation and a gift from the organizer and was mentioned in the story about the race in the local paper. I would bring my sales and organizational abilities to your organization.

Quick Learner: I have several notable accomplishments in my career. One that I am very proud of is when a friend referred me to a law firm that needed a website makeover. Since I was primarily an SEO (Search Engine Optimization) expert, revamping a website for me was new territory. I viewed this more as a consulting assignment and I had never acted as a consultant. I asked the attorneys lots of questions so I would have a better idea of what services they wanted to offer on the website, how they wanted to describe themselves, and the theme, look and feel of the website. I listened intensely and found that there was some disagreement between the lawyers, but by drilling down with questions, we were able to come to a consensus. I quickly taught myself Wordpress and created a review site for the attorneys. I worked long hours as it was a steep learning curve, and I loved every minute of it. At our review meeting, the attorneys had some comments which I incorporated. At the end of the day, they approved the website and I added extra value by maximizing their

SEO. Consulting is bringing in at least five new clients per week in the local market. That is why I am excited about this job because I will have the opportunity to work with your clients requiring website makeovers.

Project Leader: My greatest accomplishment was not only a win for the company, but it also gave me a great deal of satisfaction. I was responsible for planning and executing our company charity day where we go out into the community to do good works. I was able to recruit a team of volunteers—one from each department. They went back to brainstorm with their own groups on ideas for community service. I discovered that there were so many great ideas that we could not just pick one as we had done in years past. So, I checked with the CEO to see if we could do multiple projects with smaller teams. She was supportive. Our volunteers took ownership of being team captains for the three projects: 1) we cleaned up the downtown park, 2) we read to a first grade class, and 3) we painted the inside walls of a homeless shelter and then served food. We created a communication plan between community leaders and our own employees, and we arranged all the logistical details. I also pulled in our public relations team to ensure that the CEO was interviewed on the 6 pm local news. The bottom line is that we had 95 percent participation from employees and our post event survey showed off-the-chart ratings. Everyone who participated felt good afterwards about giving back to the community. It was also great press for the company. I felt I created and drove these community projects to fruition. I am excited about working for your event planning company because I love the challenge of creating a project plan, managing people, and paying attention to every detail.

RECAP

To answer the accomplishment question, use the STAR format and talk about what you did to make it happen. Include anything you learned along the way and mention the result—like savings, management recognition, awards, or how you involved other people to ensure it got done. Wrap it up by making a connection to the job you are applying for—it shows your excitement for the job.

What could we accomplish if we knew we could not fail?" Eleanor Roosevelt, First Lady of the U.S., diplomat and activist

Okay, your turn. Write out your answers to Question #12: "Tell me about a recent accomplishment" on the next page or on the downloadable answer template.

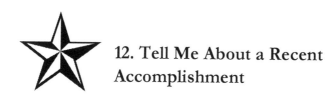

12. Tell Me About a Recent Accomplishment

The STAR Technique Template

SITUATION: Describe the *accomplishment:*

I have several notable accomplishments in my career. One that I am particularly proud of is: _____

_____

TASK: Explain what you had to do and the challenges you encountered:

_____

_____

_____

ACTION: Explain what you did to solve the problem or how you met a performance objective by describing the process, steps, talents and strengths you used:

_____

_____

_____

RESULTS: What was the outcome or bottom line result? If you have metrics, please use them. If there was a lesson learned, what was it?

_____

_____

CHAPTER 16

Question #13: Tell Me About a Time When You Failed

This question makes you wonder what failure you could possibly reveal about yourself that won't ruin your chances of getting the job. It seems like a yo-yo question. *You just asked me about my strengths and to talk about an accomplishment, and now you want me to talk about a failure. In addition, you already asked me about my weaknesses and this was uncomfortable enough!* What the interviewer is looking for is someone who learns from their mistakes. This is just like the weakness question, it is all about self-awareness, the willingness to admit your failures—what did you do wrong, what did you forget to do, or a time when you did not take appropriate action, and how you learned from it so it does not happen again.

ANSWER TIPS

Select a story where you failed and learned from it, resulting in modified behavior. You can't pick something insignificant like getting an average grade in school because you did not study enough. At the same time, it can't be something where the failure had a mega impact on the company or others. This is about a behavior (which can always be changed) versus some fatal flaw that is going to follow you around from job to job. It's those learning experiences that make you think—next time, I will do it differently. Taking ownership of what you did and how you recovered is the key.

This is a great opportunity for a STAR formatted story. As part of describing the situation, you will want to define what failure means to you in your chosen situation. For example: I think of failure as not meeting a goal, or I view failure as a communication breakdown, or I think of failure whenever I impact another person in a negative way.

Then you can go into the rest of the situation, task, action and results. Be sure to mention what you learned!

This should be a shorter answer than the standard two minutes. It can be as short as one minute—just get to the punch line quicker on what you did or did not do (which is the failure) and what your big AHA was. The AHA will be what you would have done now that you know how to handle this type of situation and what you will do going forward.

EXAMPLES

Managing Resistance: I view failure as not reading between the lines when you get objections. Early in my career, I had a project that involved people from three other departments. I assumed that once we agreed on the project plan that everyone would be on board. However, one person who had pushed back on the aggressive timeline initially, but agreed to the deadline as we walked out the door, did not deliver his piece of the project on time. Consequently, the rest of us had to pitch in and do his job. One of my biggest takeaways from the experience is to always dig further when people disagree and then commit. In speaking with the individual afterwards, I learned that he was dealing with a personal problem that required a lot of time and the pressure of coming to a consensus in the meeting just made him cave in and agree to the assignment and deadline. From that day forward, I learned to seek the "why" to any resistance from others.

Cultural Insensitivity: I view failure as cultural insensitivity. Early in my career, I got the opportunity to go to a foreign country and was very excited. I immersed myself in the language so I would be able to have some basic knowledge. What I did not do is read up on the culture. I brought my American ways with me including diving right into a business topic during our first meeting with the departmental employees. I was taken aside afterwards by the local Human Resources Director who instructed me that I must always be personal first in meetings by getting to know everyone and talking about myself. This was a big wake-up call for me. I quickly changed my ways as I had many meetings scheduled over the next 10 days. In all my travels after that, I always took the time to learn about the local culture and connect with a human resource professional to give me some pointers on how to conduct business.

RECAP

It's okay to fail. How else will you learn? For this question on failure, acknowledgement of what went wrong is paramount. It is all about failing forward because you have learned from the failure.

"Failure is the opportunity to begin again more intelligently." Henry Ford, Industrialist

Okay, your turn. Write out your answers to Question #13: "Tell me about a time when you failed" on the next page or on the downloadable answer template.

13. Tell Me About a Time When You Failed

The STAR Technique Template

SITUATION: Describe *your definition of failure and the situation:*

I view failure as:_____

_____

_____

TASK: Explain what you had to do/*did not do*:

_____

_____

_____

ACTION: Explain *why you failed in this instance:*

_____

_____

_____

RESULTS: Explain *what you learned from the failure and how it has changed the way you do things:*

_____

_____

_____

_____

CHAPTER 17

Question #14: Tell Me About a Time When You Exercised Leadership

Interviewers ask this question to learn about your leadership style and to determine if you would be a good match for their organization. If you have ever been a manager or supervisor, then this question should be an easy one as you will have a number of examples—some of them on your resume that you can expand upon. If you are not a current leader, you can focus on a time when you had to take the reins and be a leader in a group when there was none, or use a personal example—organizing any type of meeting, event, group of people etc. works great. It can be volunteer, school related, being a parent and running the PTA—it all counts. Remember, companies are always on the lookout for up and coming leaders. Even if you are a leader in training, they will want to hear what you have done in the leadership arena.

ANSWER TIPS

You will want to drag out the job requirements again and look at the leadership qualities the company is looking for. Often, the job requirements will spell it out: words like team leader, organizational skills, change management skills, decision maker, or initiative. Make sure that whatever story you tell, you pick one or several of the key words they have identified. Also, think about your leadership style and how you adapt it based upon the person you are working with. This question is perfect for a STAR formatted story.

EXAMPLES

Volunteer: I volunteered for a political campaign and four of us were assigned the job of helping to identify a campaign slogan for the candidate. At the first meeting, everyone joked about slogans used in the past which indicated to me that the group did not have experience in marketing or communications. They were all people who meant well, but they were not skilled in the task at hand. I decided to come to the next meeting to lead a brainstorming session that would get the group focused on why some slogans work and why others do not work. This began a discussion about the candidate and the importance of connecting her beliefs with the slogan. We then conducted "on the street" polls and also interviewed people she had previously worked with to analyze themes. This brainstorming and focus on research resulted in a report to the marketing committee that resulted in a slogan that we believe helped win the election because it was a true reflection of our candidate.

Merger Anxiety: Recently, our company went through a merger with another company of equal size. We knew that there would probably be some thinning out in the ranks. Rumors were circulating and making employees feel very uncomfortable which was affecting their work. Our manufacturing production line productivity levels had decreased by 25 percent due to the slowdown in actual products assembled. I knew that for my team, I needed to take corrective action. I gathered them together and asked about their concerns. After each question, I expressed both understanding and then exhibited transparency in answering the question. I think the ability to be honest and up front with people is important in situations when there is a level of uncertainty. My team thanked me for my candor. Later that afternoon, several other supervisors came to me because they had heard from their own staff that I had conducted a special meeting. Each asked if I could help them do the same. The result of talking honestly and openly decreased the noise level and the rumors. People got back to work and our productivity increased back to normal levels.

RECAP

You will have many leadership experiences in both your personal and professional lives. Often, you are not even aware that you have picked up the leadership mantle. I know when you reflect back on your own career, there will be several defining moments that make you proud. Select one and put it into a STAR format—this story will be a keeper in the brain of the interviewer.

"Leadership belongs to those who take it."
Sheryl Sandberg, COO of Facebook

Okay, your turn. Write out your answers to Question #14: "Tell me about a time when you exercised leadership" on the next page or on the downloadable answer template.

14. Tell Me About a Time When You
Exercised Leadership

The STAR Technique Template

SITUATION: Describe the *leadership* opportunity you faced:

_____

_____

TASK: Explain what *leadership* challenges you encountered:

_____

_____

_____

ACTION: Explain *what leadership skills you used* to solve the problem:

_____

_____

_____

RESULTS: What was the outcome or bottom line result? If you have metrics, please use them. If there was a lesson learned, what was it?

_____

_____

_____

_____

CHAPTER 18

Question #15: What Do You Expect to be Doing in Five Years?

This is a question about ambition and motivation to determine whether they want to make an investment in you. Do you know enough about their career paths to discuss where you want to be? We know that careers zig and zag, but for this question, assume you are staying with this company. You will definitely exhibit loyalty by talking about being there in five years.

ANSWER TIPS

It would be ideal if in your research you discovered the different levels and positions in the company. This would help you understand the typical career progression and where five years should lead you. The inside track could come from someone who is working there now who could elaborate. If not, you should have a general understanding of the career path progression that you have chosen. The interviewer will want to know that you have a plan and how their company fits into that plan. For example, if you are in marketing you start out as an assistant brand manager, then become a brand manager, move to marketing director and then the top spot as VP of Marketing. If you are currently an assistant brand manager, you know that in the next five years you want to be a brand manager. I can tell you from my experience as an interviewer, many job seekers are just applying for everything that is out there. But, if you are serious about a company, you will know exactly where you are headed in your career.

The focus of your answer should be on personal development. Talk about the skills you will be using or learning on the job and the responsibilities you would like to take on. Your response can't be too general which sounds canned; then again it can't be too specific because if they don't have the position you describe, you are out of the running.

EXAMPLES

No experience: In five years, I will be as dedicated and motivated as I am today and hope to have achieved more responsibility over time with the company.

Mid level experience: In five years, I will have increased my project management and soft skills to be able to manage others in a supervisory role. I enjoy managing projects and teaching and mentoring others so they can succeed and reach their full potential. I would welcome the opportunity to be a part of your formal mentoring program.

Mid level experience: I want to be making a difference in the sales group of your company by helping to secure new clients and adding to your terrific reputation as a leader within the insurance industry, thus contributing to the company's bottom line.

Experienced hire: I relish having a reputation as an expert in xyz. I want to work where I'll have opportunities to further develop my knowledge, skills and talent, take on challenging projects, and work with great people who always push me to be better. This company has one of the best reputations in the industry and this is why I would love to build a career here.

If you know the career titles in the organization: I know that within five years, I should be on track to becoming a manager. I know that with the company's 'promote from within' policy, that I would be given challenges and opportunities to prove myself worthy of such a promotion.

RECAP

Throughout your career, it is critical to define your career progression and to measure yourself against those goals. How else will you know that you are making progress? Most interviewers will ask where you see yourself in five years. Of course, they want you to stay with them since they will make a training investment in you and the organization may have to pay a recruiting fee. Try to find out the career path within that company through contacts or via an Internet search. At the very least, know what promotions you can anticipate in your chosen field. Be honest, ambitious, yet humble.

"The future depends on what you do today."
Mahatma Gandhi, Leader

Okay, your turn. Write out your answers to Question #15: "What do you expect to be doing in five years?" on the next page or on the downloadable answer template.

15. What Do You Expect to be Doing in Five Years?

ASSUMPTION: You are going to stay with this company and follow their career progression. Going into the interview, you must know what the general career path titles are in the specialization you have chosen. Getting inside knowledge of titles is preferable.

In five years, I will be: _____

_____

_____

_____

_____

_____

There should be a sentence within your statement that complements the company.

Example: I know that within five years, I should be on track to becoming a manager. I know with the company's 'promote from within' policy, that I would be given challenges and opportunities to prove myself worthy of such a promotion.

Here, the individual knows the company's career path and is aware that in five years she would probably be a manager, and she compliments the company by mentioning its promote from within policy.

CHAPTER 19

Question #16: Why Should We Hire You?

There are different versions of this question such as: why are you the best candidate or what value do you feel you bring? Interviewers ask the question because they want to hear how well you can impress them. How articulate are you about yourself? If not you—then who? This question can be answered as a summary statement that combines your qualifications, the research you have done on the company, and what you have heard during the interview relative to the job and their needs. Think of it as closing the sale. What are the features and the benefits you can offer; what are your differentiators? It must be strong and convincing and all about the company's needs—not yours.

ANSWER TIPS

Job candidates have told me they want to work for me because they like me, they really, really want the job, it sounds like a cool job, or they want to get their foot in the door of a large company. No, no, no! Not appropriate—it is not about you, it is about them. Remember, it is about the abilities you have to offer them. Take a look at your branding statement four boxes worksheet. You circled skills and characteristics that matched the key or required job description requirements. You will want to focus on those areas for your answer. Dazzle the interviewer with three messages in under two minutes:

1. You can do the work (based upon your skill set) and deliver excellent results

2. You fit into their culture

3. You are unique

If the interviewer talked about a problem they are facing and that is why they are hiring, be sure to highlight the skills you would use to solve it.

Avoid using words that are overused—great team player, hard working, trustworthy, reliable, and caring.

End with a question: do you think the qualities and skills I have are what you are looking for? At this point, they may ask you some more questions or merely answer yes. You want to leave them with no questions about your capabilities.

EXAMPLES

No experience: I'm a quick learner and even though I am not experienced as a medical office receptionist, I'm a stickler for patient care. I have been in and out of doctor and dentist offices all my life. I know that often the receptionist is the first contact a patient makes and people make decisions based on the friendliness of the doctor's office staff. I truly enjoy people and had a great experience as a theme park greeter where we learned customer service principles and were observed in action to become even better. I would bring that level of enthusiasm and outstanding patient care to your office and I think this position is a great fit for me. Do you think the qualities and skills I have are what you are looking for?

Experienced hire. From our conversation, it sounds as if you are looking for someone to come in to convert your patient paper records to electronic records by June of this year. I believe that with the experience I've had in assisting four other medical practices to successfully migrate their files to the same technology platform your office will be using, I would do an excellent job for you in the time frame required. In addition, my level of energy and passion for teaching technology will lessen the stress on your staff who need to learn the new system. I look forward to the challenge. Do you think the qualities and skills I have are what you are looking for?

Experienced hire. I think you should hire me for my experience in the telecommunications industry where I managed a call center overseas which utilized both my organizational and coaching skills. You indicated that your call center turnover is at an all time high. I have helped improve two other call centers by re-engineering their schedules, providing proper breaks for individuals, rewriting scripts that were customer focused, monitoring individual calls, and providing immediate coaching to improve customer service. In both cases, turnover decreased by 10 percent and sales increased by 20 percent. I appreciate the challenge you have because turnover creates issues with morale and affects the bottom line. I would truly enjoy the opportunity to work with you. Do you think the qualities and skills I have are what you are looking for?

RECAP

Use a mini summary of your abilities, experience and results tied to the job requirements. Also, please note that the interviewer may not even ask this question. Even if they don't, you must end the interview with your strong summary statement before you walk out the door.

"You have only one thing to sell in life, and that's yourself." Henry Kravis, Co-founder Kohlberg, Kravis, Roberts & Co.

Okay, your turn. Write out your answers to Question #16: "Why should we hire you?" on the next page or on the downloadable answer template.

16. Why Should We Hire You?

CLOSING THE SALE: This is a *two minute* summary statement that combines your qualifications, the research you have done on the company, and what you have heard during the interview relative to the job needs. Here are some sentence starters:

I'm a quick learner and even though I am not experienced as a

_____

I'm a _____

_____

_____

_____

From our conversations, it sounds as if you are looking for someone to _____

_____

_____

I think you should hire me for my experience in the _____

industry_____

_____

_____

Remember, it is a mini recap of your abilities, experience and results tied to the job requirements.

Be sure to end with the question: Do you think the qualities and skills I have are what you are looking for?

CHAPTER 20

Question #17: Why Do You Want to Work for Us?

I know you may be thinking, why is the interviewer asking this question? It seems like a no-brainer. You want to work for them because this is the perfect opportunity for you! While that can be your inner dialogue, it is not appropriate to scream this from the rafters. The interviewer wants to know if you have done your homework on the company and the industry. We discussed this in Chapter 1—do your research. What is it about the company that makes you want to join them? This is the complementary question to why you; now it is why us?

ANSWER TIPS

Be armed with your information on the company and the industry. What are the two-three reasons you want to work for them? Perhaps it is something about their culture or mission statement; do you believe in their products; are they one of the best companies to work for; is their financial performance stellar? Your answer will reflect that you have thought about the kind of company with which you want to be associated. This is not a STAR story—all you need is two-three sentences at the most.

EXAMPLES

Recent Press: Based on research I've done, your company is an industry leader with an excellent reputation. Recently, the press has written a number of articles on the quality of the products you manufacture with an all U.S. labor force. Being an Army veteran and having served in Iraq, I appreciate the dedication you have to manufacturing in the U.S. I want to be associated with such a high-minded organization.

Honors: Based on my research, I am impressed that over the last five years, you have grabbed top honors in being one of the Top 100 small companies in our city due to your technology innovation and growth in revenues. I know that I would be an asset and make a contribution immediately.

Prior Employee: A friend of mine worked here for a number of years and continues to rave about the strong leadership and outstanding co-workers. So, I know this is an excellent place to work. It is all about the people that makes me want to join your company.

Mission: Based on my research, I have discovered that your mission to provide doctors with medical supplies and send them out in chartered planes when disaster strikes is a mission I believe in strongly, too. I would love the opportunity to be a part of such a worthwhile effort.

Firsthand experience: My two children go to school here and I have been very satisfied with the quality of education they are receiving from the teachers. I know several teachers who work here and they talk about the great camaraderie and outstanding administration. I think this would be a great place to start my teaching career.

RECAP

Find something that has impressed you about the company, identify the source, and tell them why you want to work for them in under one minute. Show your enthusiasm about the prospect of working for this company. You aren't just another job applicant willing to take any job!

"The only way to do great work is to love what you do. If you haven't found it, keep looking. Don't settle."
Steve Jobs, Co-founder Apple Inc.

Okay, your turn. Write out your answers to Question #17: "Why do you want to work for us?" on the next page or on the downloadable answer template.

17. Why Do You Want to Work for Us?

Based upon your company research and understanding of the job, what are the two-three reasons you want to work for them?

_____

_____

_____

_____

_____

_____

_____

_____

_____

_____

CHAPTER 21

Question #18: What Is Your Current Salary?

This is one of those questions that needs finesse. Interviewers ask the salary question because they want to know if you know your worth and, let's face it, it gives them knowledge to negotiate the salary. You don't really want to answer the question because you don't want to be boxed into a low salary. For instance, your salary might not be market-based because your current company does not pay well or you work in a nonprofit or a start-up. Or, your salary could be too high and turn off an interviewer because they can't afford you.

ANSWER TIPS

Part of your pre-work is to look up the company salary ranges on Glassdoor.com or Payscale.com. Knowing this information will help you finesse the salary question. You really want to avoid telling them your current salary because this may be the only shot you have of giving yourself a raise. Over the last 10 years, U.S. companies have barely given cost of living raises.

There are several ways to handle the question:

1. Tell them what your current salary range is (never the exact number) but add a caveat to explain why it is low or high.

2. Don't reveal your current salary, but instead push to talk about the range of salary you are looking for. If you have done your salary research, you should know the salary ranges for the company or the industry norm for the job. If you do not know the salary range, then simply ask the interviewer what it is.

3. Don't ever pad your salary. It is amazing how much recruiters and human resource professionals know about what other companies pay.

4. Recruiters and companies should not ask to verify your salary through tax return verification. It is a bullying technique in my book. Your response should be that you are not comfortable providing this information as it is a family return or it is simply too much personal information.

EXAMPLES

The bold answer: I believe my current salary is not reflective of the responsibilities here. Can you tell me what the salary range is so I can give you an idea of what I am looking for?

If you are underpaid: I believe I am currently underpaid, so my salary is not a reflection of my skills. I am looking for (state a salary range).

If you are overpaid: Salary is not an issue for me if the job is right and I am the best candidate. What have you budgeted for this job?

Salary range: I am earning in the mid five figures (that sounds like $45-60K) or I am earning in the high five figures with a bonus.

RECAP

Stating what you are looking for in the way of salary is always best by using a range yourself. For instance, if the company salary range is $75,000 – $100,000 and your current salary is $80,000, you might want to say I am looking for $85,000 – $90,000. The likelihood of getting $100,000, the top of the range, is slim.

If the salary range they have quoted is below your minimum, be honest and state the range you want.

Remember, you want to establish yourself as a highly competent individual who is well-suited for the position—as well as a competitive salary.

Salary is a very personal benchmark. For some people, salary is more important than the job itself, and for others the job is of paramount importance and the salary is secondary. Determine which is more important to you, and this will help you answer the salary question.

"We do not go to work only to earn an income, but to find meaning in our lives. What we do is a large part of what we are."
Alan Ryan, British political philosopher

Okay, your turn. Write out your answers to Question #18: "What is your current salary?" on the next page or on the downloadable answer template.

18. What Is Your Current Salary?

Know what the company salary ranges are either through someone who works there or do research on glassdoor.com or payscale.com.

Some tips:

1. Do not divulge your exact current salary amount. It is better to provide a range of salary and explain why it is low or high.

2. If you do not know the company's salary range, ask the interviewer. Then, respond to the question of whether that range would be appropriate or not.

3. Do not pad your salary.

4. Do not submit tax return verification of your salary.

EXAMPLES:

If you are BOLD: There is no comparison to my current job, and I believe my current salary is not reflective of the responsibilities here. Can you tell me what the salary range is so I can give you an idea of what I am looking for?

If you are UNDERPAID: I believe I am currently underpaid, so my salary is not a reflection of my skills. I am looking for (state a salary range).

If you are OVERPAID: Salary is not an issue for me if the job is right and I am the best candidate. What have you budgeted for this job?

If you want to provide the RANGE: I am earning in the mid five figures, etc.

Write your answer:

_____

_____

_____

_____

_____

_____

_____

CHAPTER 22

Question #19: Don't You Think You Are Overqualified?

This can be a question that makes you gulp because it makes you wonder—if they thought you were overqualified, why did they bother asking you to come in to interview? And, for those of you over age 50, it may be code words in your mind for "you're too old" and smacks of ageism. Stay out of that negative zone; it does not mean they are rejecting you. The reason behind the question is: interviewers want to know if you are going to be bored and leave when a better opportunity arises or they may assume they won't be able to afford you. Take ownership because you may have said something during the interview that sparked the question. Interviewers have so many candidates these days that are overqualified because of the economy, and they can't afford the boredom factor turnover.

ANSWER TIPS

Let's recognize the elephant in the room and tackle it head on with a response that is both honest and shows your determination in getting the job. You definitely want to convince the interviewer that hiring you will be an advantage to them.

Do not lessen your experience or credentials by dumbing them down. Be proud and take credit for what you have done. Highlight your experience and how it will benefit the company. Put your commitment and dedication to the company on the line. Be sure to state that you want to stay with the company for a long time. If you have stayed for a long time at other companies, be sure to point that out again.

Two strengths you can focus on because they come with experience are that you are proficient at what you do and are a great mentor to other employees. In addition, knowing what you want at this stage means you are dedicated and ready to roll up your sleeves. So, they save time by not having to train you. You are instantly productive.

EXAMPLES

Mentor: While my qualifications are extensive, every company has different processes. I am a continuous learner eager to understand different approaches, and I enjoy working with new people. My broad experience makes me an ideal mentor for younger workers. I am always dedicated and committed to the companies I join and I stay for many years. (Note: I never used the word "overqualified").

Work fulfillment: I have enjoyed this kind of work for many years and want to continue to do it as I get a great sense of fulfillment from it and certainly would not find it boring. I really do want this job and appreciate the opportunity to work for such a terrific company; my intention is to stay for a long time.

Commitment: I am confident that I can perform this job and begin to contribute immediately knowing that with such a great company, other opportunities will open up along the way. I definitely am willing to make a long-term commitment.

Skills: I do have an extensive background and have received great training in software design at my other jobs. This is an investment of time and money that you do not need to make in me as I am ready to hit the ground running. I am committed to the long haul.

Knows Self: I realize that I was a marketing product manager in my last role, and I appreciate the knowledge I gained from supervising others. However, I've decided that my sweet spot of experience is developing brands and being on the creative side. That is exactly what this job offers. It isn't about falling off the career ladder or going backwards. It is about a great career match and bringing my wealth of creative branding experience to a company on the leading edge and being productive for a long, long time.

RECAP

It is disheartening to get rejected due to age. Keep in mind that you don't need every job—you need one job. An employer who rejects you due to over-qualification is the loser, not you! Besides, who wants to work for a company that does not value the more experienced population? Keep it short and sweet—be sure to mention a few strengths that don't require training and state your commitment to the company.

"Make a total commitment to your company, your job, your career. Uncommitted people have no future."
Brian Tracy, Author

Okay, your turn. Write out your answers to Question #19: "Don't you think you are overqualified?" on the next page or on the downloadable answer template.

19. Don't You Think You Are Overqualified?

Highlight your experience and how it will benefit the company. End with a statement that reflects your commitment and dedication to the company and that you are there for the long-term.

Write your answer:

_____

_____

_____

_____

_____

_____

CHAPTER 23

Question #20: Do You Have Any Questions to Ask Me?

This is what I call the last dance question. You definitely want to ask a few questions. Saying that you have no questions is a deal breaker. The interviewer wants to know that you have an interest in joining them and that this hasn't been a 30-40 minute waste of their time. They want to also know you have been listening and that you have questions related to ensuring the job is a right fit for you.

First, let's talk about the questions to never, ever ask. Never ask about salary, benefits, personal time off, maternity/paternity leave, etc. Those questions are best saved for once you have a job offer.

ANSWER TIPS

Hopefully, you have been jotting down some points to follow-up on things the interviewer has said that you want to probe further. As a failsafe, be sure to have several questions, prepared in advance, in your back pocket.

Questions fall into four major categories:

1. Questions about the job or role
2. Questions about the company
3. Questions about the interviewer
4. Questions about the decision process

EXAMPLES

Job or role:

- What do you feel it takes to be successful in this job? This indicates you want to be successful in the job.

- What is the biggest challenge in this job? This shows you are ready to take on the challenge.

- What are the three things you would want me to accomplish in the first 90 days? Super question showing you want to contribute right away and making it sound like you are already invested in solving their problems and contributing immediately.

- How does this position help the company achieve its goals? This is a great question because it shows the interviewer that you are thinking about the bigger picture.

- And, here is my bold question to ask: How do you feel about my experience in filling this job? Yes, it is an in-their-face question, but it may get the interviewer to talk about any reservations and provide you the opportunity to address objections. It also signals to the interviewer that you are open to feedback and want to build self-awareness.

Company: Particularly if you were not able to find information during your research.

- How would you describe the company's culture?

- What company values do you see exhibited daily?

Both questions emphasize the importance of culture and values to you.

Interviewer:

- Why did you choose to work here, and what keeps you here?

I love this question because you will hear a lot about the culture of the company, the challenges, the people, etc. And, quite frankly, the interviewer will be flattered you asked. It also shows you are interested in them as a person.

Decision Process:

- What are the next steps/timeframes?

This question needs to be asked before the end of the interview so you will understand how long it will be before they contact you. This will allow you to time your follow-up appropriately.

RECAP

The worst thing you can do when an interviewer asks if you have any questions is answer with: "No, you've answered everything." Be engaging and ask one of the above questions. At the very least, ask the next steps/timeframe question.

"Ask the right questions if you're to find the right answers." Vanessa Redgrave, Actor

Okay, your turn. Write out your answers to Question #20: "Do you have any questions to ask me?" on the next page or on the downloadable answer template.

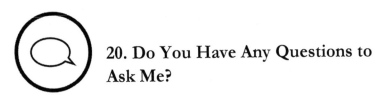

20. Do You Have Any Questions to Ask Me?

Appropriate questions fall into four major categories:

1. Job or role

2. Company

3. Interviewer

4. Decision Process – this is a MUST question.

Write your questions for the interviewer:

_____

_____

_____

_____

_____

_____

_____

Final question is: What are the next steps/timeframe?

****

Congratulations, you made it through all the Top 20 questions. You can now review your own answers, modify and sharpen them and then REHEARSE.

CHAPTER 24

Bonus Interview Tips

Are you ready for some bonus tips? Here are my Top 10 interview bonus tips for you to consider:

1. **Conduct a mock interview** with a coach, friend, or family member. The more you rehearse, the more you will remember. My favorite trick is to do it in front of a mirror. Every time you see yourself in the mirror talking means you have gotten to the point where you have a ready answer.

2. **Bring extra copies of your resume** in case you wind up interviewing with others who have not seen it. I have been excited about a candidate and asked them if they minded talking with another person and forgotten the resume.

3. **Dress for success.** See if you can find out what the dress code is. If you don't know the company attire... a suit for men and women is perfectly fine. When in doubt, dress up. This is the first 30 second rule: you never have a second chance to make a great first impression.

4. **Test drive and find the location.** Always time how long it is going to take to get to the office and figure out where you will park. You don't want the added stress of getting lost.

5. **Arrive early.** Arriving early means 10-15 minutes before your allotted time. Take time to catch your breath, use the restroom, and watch how the employees treat each other.

6. **Cultivate the right mindset.** Accept your nervousness and embrace it. Appreciate the value you bring to the employer. Visualize a successful interview. View the interview as a testing

ground to determine if you want the job, and the worst case scenario is you don't get it—so view it as great practice for your interviewing skills.

7. **Greet everyone with respect.** I was once walking a candidate to the elevator and when the doors closed, the receptionist pulled me over and told me about the poor behavior he exhibited towards her. Needless to say, I did not hire the person.

8. **Be your authentic self.** You cannot pretend to be someone else. You are unique and you want to be honest and forthright. A big smile and a strong handshake go a long way.

9. **Take notes.** It is perfectly okay to take notes as you will want to jot down questions to ask later or write down a reminder for yourself to mention to the interviewer. Just seek permission up front by asking if it is alright with the interviewer if you take notes. Everyone will say yes. We are talking about one to two word notes, not a novel! By taking notes, it indicates to the interviewer that you are serious about the job.

10. **Thank you note.** Did you know that only 10 percent of job candidates send a follow-up thank you note? Always, always send a thank you note to the interviewer for their time and again express interest in the job and the company. Do this within 24 hours. Do it even if you don't want the job because you never know from a networking perspective who the interviewer knows. A quick e-mail or handwritten note makes a great impression.

CONCLUSION

I know that some of the tips discussed above are common sense. But, if you get brilliant on these basics, you will have a strong foundation for your interviews.

After every interview, I recommend you do the following four actions:

1. Dash off that thank you note to the interviewer or interviewers.
2. Analyze what you did well and what you would change next time.
3. Relax and treat yourself to something special.
4. Give yourself a pat on the back for doing the best you could.

I hope you have taken advantage of capturing your notes and stories in the Companion Guide fill-in-the-blank answer templates. By taking the time to think and write out your responses in advance, you are 99% more prepared than most job candidates because you now know the majority of questions that will be asked and you have prepared your STAR stories. Practice does make perfect, so please do it with a coach, a friend, or a family member and in private in front of a mirror. It will settle some of the nervousness, too. Congratulations for putting in the time.

Here are my final thoughts for you. Remember to be who you are... there is no perfect answer. There is only your authentic answer. Listen intently and read between the lines of what the interviewer is saying or asking. Be in the moment—pause, think, and then respond. Keep your energy high because most employers do not hire on skill alone. Your enthusiasm, communication, interpersonal skills, and confidence are just as important. You are unique and any company would be fortunate to have you as part of their team.

Wishing you the best of career success!

About the Author

Katie Weiser is a speaker, author, career coach, consultant, and workshop leader. She is the owner of Katie Weiser Coaching in Augusta, Georgia. She works one-on-one with individuals to help them make career decisions that will lead to living the career of their dreams.

In her 30 years of experience at Deloitte Consulting, she worked with CEO's, business leaders, and human resource professionals. She interviewed, hired, developed, coached and managed professionals at all levels. Her leadership positions included Global Director of Training and Development and Global Director of Alumni Relations. In her alumni position, she created and implemented a career transition program and personally worked with over 500 professionals to assist them with their job searches.

Katie is credentialed by the International Coach Federation as a Professional Certified Coach (PCC). She graduated from The Institute for Professional Excellence in Coaching and has a BA in Psychology from Hunter College of The City University of New York.

She spent most of her career in New York and Atlanta. She and her husband, Allan, live in Augusta, Georgia and Ocala, Florida.

Katie is the proud daughter of a U.S. Army WWII, Korea and Vietnam veteran who passed away in 2012 at the age of 91. She traveled and moved every few years as a child and continues to enjoy traveling today.

Download your FREE Companion Guide Answer Templates

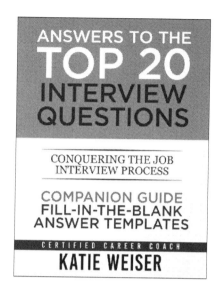

Are you worried about being tongue tied during the interview? Use the super-easy downloadable fill-in-the-blank COMPANION GUIDE ANSWER TEMPLATES for each of the Top 20 questions. Each template provides prompts to help you complete your own answers.

Your key benefits are:

- Knowledge of the prospective questions will give you a head start over the other candidates.

- The simple act of writing out your own answers will help you remember what you want to say.

- Advance preparation will reduce your anxiety and build up your confidence.

- Your own answers captured on paper will enable you to rehearse and evaluate how well you are prepared.

Go to <u>katieweisercoaching.com/top20/</u> to request your FREE downloadable fill-in-the-blank answer templates now!

85295911R00069

Made in the USA
San Bernardino, CA
18 August 2018